# Journey of a Bar of Chocolate

## John Malam

Raintree

**www.raintreepublishers.co.uk**
Visit our website to find out more information about Raintree books.

**To order:**
☎ Phone 0845 6044371
🖹 Fax +44 (0) 1865 312263
🖳 Email myorders@raintreepublishers.co.uk

Customers from outside the UK please telephone +44 1865 312262

Raintree is an imprint of Capstone Global Library Limited, a company incorporated in England and Wales having its registered office at 7 Pilgrim Street, London, EC4V 6LB – Registered company number: 6695582

Text © Capstone Global Library Limited 2012
First published in hardback in 2012
Paperback edition first published in 2013
The moral rights of the proprietor have been asserted.

Edited by Dan Nunn and Diyan Leake
Designed by Cynthia Della-Rovere
Original illustrations © Capstone Global Library Ltd 2012
Illustrated by Capstone Global Library Ltd
Picture research by Mica Brancic
Production by Alison Parsons
Originated by Capstone Global Library Ltd
Printed and bound in China by Leo Paper Products Ltd

ISBN 978 1 406 23934 8 (hardback)
16 15 14 13 12
10 9 8 7 6 5 4 3 2 1

ISBN 978 1 406 23941 6 (paperback)
17 16 15
10 9 8 7 6 5 4 3

**British Library Cataloguing in Publication Data**
Malam, John, 1957–
Journey of a chocolate bar.
641.3'374-dc22
A full catalogue record for this book is available from the British Library.

**Acknowledgements**
The author and publishers are grateful to the following for permission to reproduce copyright material: Alamy pp. 5 (© Beepstock), 6 (© Marion Kaplan), 10 (© Simon Rawles), 17 (© Bon Appetit), 18 (© John Warburton-Lee Photograph/Camilla Watson), 24 (© Bon Appetit), 25 (© Eightfish), 26 (© Rob Walls); © Capstone Publishers (Karon Dubke) p. 27; Corbis pp. 12 (© Olivier Polet), 14 (Reuters/© Luc Gnago), 22 (Sygma/© Richard Melloul), 28 (© image 100); Corbis Sygma (© Annebicque Bernard) p. 20; Getty Images pp. 11 (© AFP Photo/Issouf Sanogo), 15 (© AFP Photo/Sia Kambou), 16 (© AFP Photo/Dominique Faget), 21 (© Bloomberg/Frantzesco Kangaris); Shutterstock pp. 1 (© Picsfive), 3 (© Feng Yu), 4 top (© Luis Santos), 4 bottom (© Rafa Irusta), 4 right (© Feng Yu), 8 (© XuRa), 9 (© Dr Morley Read), 13 (© Maceofoto), 19 (© Baloncici), 23 (© Subbotina Anna), 29 (© Picsfive), 31 top (© XuRa), 31 bottom (© Baloncici).

Cover photographs of chocolate flowing (© Mikael Damkier), a chocolate bar (© Picsfive), and raw cocoa beans (© Pierre-Yves Babelon) reproduced with permission of Shutterstock.

Every effort has been made to contact copyright holders of material reproduced in this book. Any omissions will be rectified in subsequent printings if notice is given to the publisher.

# Contents

Some words are shown in bold, **like this**. You can find out what they mean by looking in the Glossary.

# Who likes chocolate?

Most people like to eat chocolate. It comes in lots of different forms. People use chocolate to make cakes and biscuits, or milkshakes, hot drinks, and ice cream.

Best of all, chocolate can be made into bars of chocolate or sweets such as chocolate buttons, coins, or eggs. Where does chocolate come from? How is it made into bars? Read on to find out!

# Where cocoa beans grow

Chocolate is made from cocoa beans. The beans grow inside **pods** on cocoa trees. These trees only grow in hot, wet parts of the world, near to the **equator**.

Most cocoa trees in West Africa grow on small family farms.

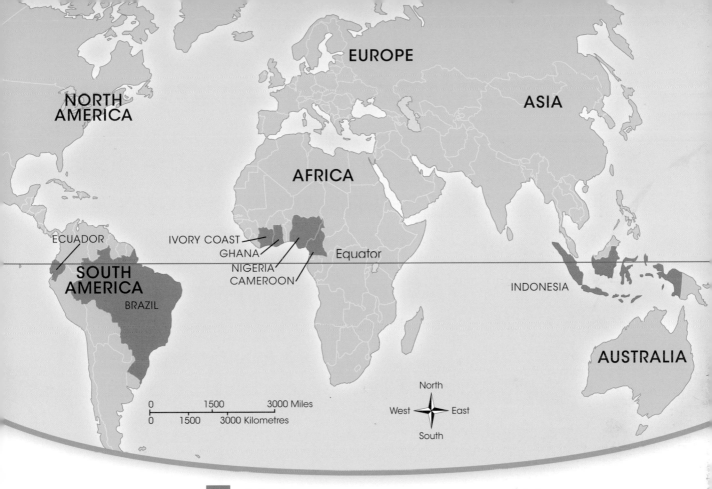

EUROPE

NORTH AMERICA

ASIA

AFRICA

ECUADOR

IVORY COAST
GHANA
NIGERIA
CAMEROON
Equator

SOUTH AMERICA

BRAZIL

INDONESIA

AUSTRALIA

0    1500    3000 Miles
0    1500    3000 Kilometres

North
West — East
South

■ Main cocoa-growing countries

Most cocoa trees grow in West Africa, South America, and parts of Asia. More than two million farms grow cocoa trees in West Africa. That's a lot of trees! A lot of cocoa beans grow on them to make chocolate.

# Pods filled with beans

Cocoa **pods** grow on cocoa trees. The pods grow from the tree trunks and the main branches. Each tree makes 20 to 30 big pods a year.

A fully grown cocoa pod can be as big as a pineapple.

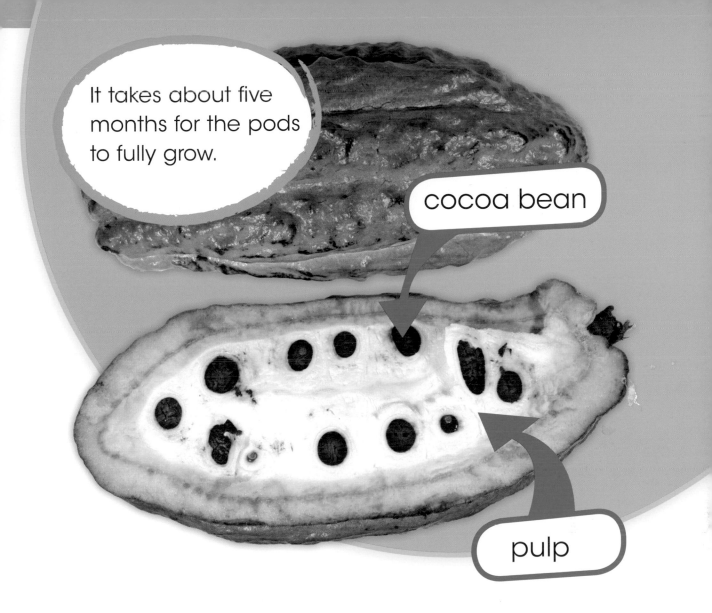

It takes about five months for the pods to fully grow.

cocoa bean

pulp

There are 50 to 60 seeds inside each cocoa pod. These are the cocoa beans. They are tucked inside a layer of white **pulp**. The pulp looks like cotton wool.

# Harvesting the pods

Farmers cut the **ripe** cocoa pods off the trees.

In West Africa, farmers **harvest** cocoa **pods** between October and January every year. They cut them off or knock them down with sticks. They take the pods back to their farms and split them open.

The farmers scoop the beans and **pulp** out by hand. They pile it into big heaps. They cover the heaps with banana leaves and leave them in the sun. This starts to give the beans their chocolate flavour.

# Drying in the sun

The **pulp** turns to liquid in the heaps. It drains away after about a week. Only the beans are left. Farmers spread the beans over mats or tables.

The farmers leave the cocoa beans to dry in the sun.

The dried beans are put into big sacks.

The farmers turn the beans over and over every day. This is to make sure they dry right through. It takes about a week for the beans to dry out. They shrink and become hard.

# Transporting the beans

The dried cocoa beans are taken to a **port**. The sacks are stored in **warehouses** there until it is time to load them on to **cargo ships**.

These sacks of cocoa beans are being taken out of a warehouse.

Forklift trucks move the sacks of cocoa beans from the warehouse to a ship. Cranes lift the sacks on to the ship. Some ships carry the beans loose – millions and millions of them!

# Roasting the beans

**Cargo ships** take the cocoa beans to countries around the world. When they arrive, the ships are unloaded. The beans are taken to chocolate **factories**.

These sacks of cocoa beans have come from a country in West Africa.

Roasting turns the beans dark brown.

The beans are cleaned at the chocolate factory. Then they are roasted in a very hot oven. Roasting brings out more of the chocolate taste in the beans.

# Removing the shells

Rollers crush the roasted beans. Rolling cracks open the hard shells of the beans. The pieces of bean inside the shells are called **nibs**.

These beans are being crushed by hand.

shells

beans

nibs

A blast of air blows away the broken shells and leaves the nibs behind. Gardeners buy the bits of broken shell! They put it on top of soil so that the soil does not dry out.

# Cocoa mass

The cocoa **nibs** are **ground** into a sticky paste called cocoa mass. Cocoa mass has **cocoa butter** and specks of cocoa in it. The cocoa mass is pressed to separate the cocoa butter and the cocoa.

The cocoa nibs are ground in machines like these.

Cocoa mass is runny when it comes out of the machine.

Pressing forces the cocoa butter out of the cocoa mass. The cocoa is poured into **moulds**. Then it is left to go hard and become blocks of solid cocoa.

# Becoming milk chocolate

The blocks of solid cocoa are heated up. The cocoa melts and becomes a thick, brown liquid. It looks like lovely chocolate, but pure cocoa has a very, very **bitter** taste.

Chocolate does not taste nice before sugar is added to it.

Milk and cocoa butter are stirred into liquid cocoa to make it smooth.

Sugar is added to the cocoa to make it taste sweet. Cocoa, milk, **cocoa butter**, and sugar are the **ingredients** in **milk chocolate**.

# Bars of chocolate

Bars of chocolate are made in **moulds**. A machine pours the warm, runny chocolate into them. This happens very quickly.

Hundreds of moulds are filled every minute of the day!

These bars are ready to come out of their moulds.

The filled moulds are put into a big fridge. The chocolate cools down. When the chocolate is hard, the moulds are emptied. The bars of chocolate come out of the moulds.

# Into the shops

The bars of chocolate are wrapped and packed into boxes. Then off they go to shops and supermarkets for customers to buy.

There are lots of different bars of chocolate to choose from!

Customers pay the shops and the shops pay the company that made the chocolate. In turn, the chocolate company pays the farmers who grew the cocoa beans.

# Chocolate – a special treat!

As you bite into a chocolate bar, think about the long journey it has had. Remember what it takes to turn cocoa beans into yummy chocolate.

A chocolate bar is a special treat.

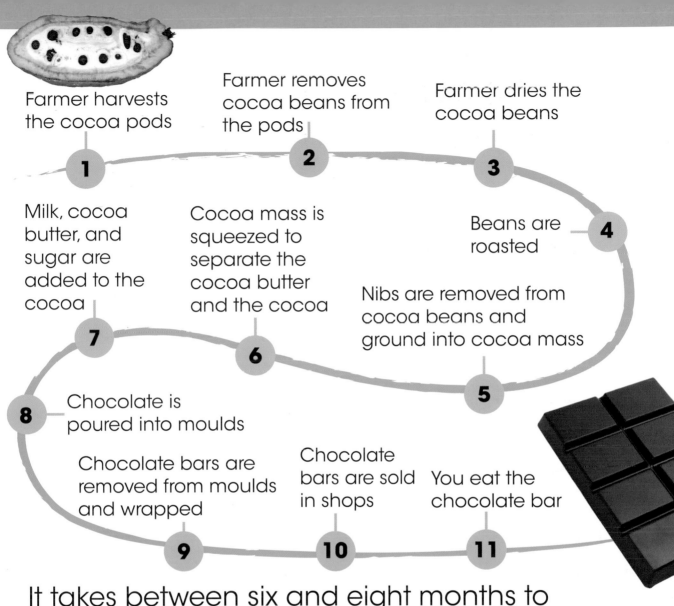

Farmer harvests the cocoa pods

Farmer removes cocoa beans from the pods

Farmer dries the cocoa beans

1

2

3

Milk, cocoa butter, and sugar are added to the cocoa

Cocoa mass is squeezed to separate the cocoa butter and the cocoa

Beans are roasted

4

Nibs are removed from cocoa beans and ground into cocoa mass

7

6

5

Chocolate is poured into moulds

8

Chocolate bars are removed from moulds and wrapped

Chocolate bars are sold in shops

You eat the chocolate bar

9

10

11

It takes between six and eight months to grow cocoa **pods** and make them into chocolate. Somewhere in the world, a farmer is growing cocoa beans right now. They may become the chocolate you eat one day!

# Glossary

**bitter**  tastes sour and strong, not sweet. Strong coffee without sugar tastes bitter.

**cargo ship**  ship that carries goods rather than passengers. The goods are known as cargo.

**cocoa butter**  yellowish-white fatty matter that comes from cocoa beans

**equator**  an imaginary line around the middle of the Earth

**factory**  building where things are made

**ground**  crushed to a powder or a paste

**harvest**  gather in fruit, vegetables, or grains that are ripe

**ingredient**  part used in a mixture

**milk chocolate**  a type of chocolate that has milk in it

**mould**  hollow container. When liquid is poured into a mould, it forms the shape of the mould after it becomes a solid.

**nib**  part that is inside a cocoa bean that is used to make chocolate

**pod**  fruit of the cocoa tree. A cocoa pod has cocoa beans inside it.

**port**  place where ships sail to and from

**pulp**  soft matter inside a cocoa pod

**ripe**  fully grown and ready for picking

**warehouse**  building where things are stored

# Chocolate quiz

1. What is chocolate made from? (see page 6)

2. When are cocoa pods harvested in West Africa? (see page 10)

3. What are the pieces inside cocoa beans called? (see page 18)

4. What is added to cocoa to make it taste sweet? (see page 23)

5. What are bars of chocolate made in? (see page 24)

# Find out more

You can find facts, figures, photos, and videos about chocolate on this website: **www.thestoryofchocolate.com**

This clip showing how chocolate is grown and prepared was filmed in Costa Rica, Central America: **www.youtube.com/watch?v=fiMjr3Rwdjs**

**Answers to quiz**

1. cocoa beans, 2. between October and January, 3. nibs, 4. sugar, 5. moulds

# Index